I Like You More Than...

The other day,
I realized something remarkable...

Of all the little joys in the world, I like you
more than every one of them combined.

It's quite astounding. I like you more than...

...a sunrise filtering through the curtains
and taking that first morning stretch.

I like you more than
watching squirrels
eat their breakfast
and birds flying by.

You're more wonderful
than tiny dogs in knit sweaters.
And cats purring in the sun.

I like you more than
melted butter on toast.
And more than that
first crunchy bite...

I like you more than
the gentle swirl of tea and
the sound of a stirring spoon.

You're as brilliant
as bells on bikes.
As caring as a bus,
stopping for two more.

I like you more than butterflies on flowers,

more than seeds beginning to sprout.

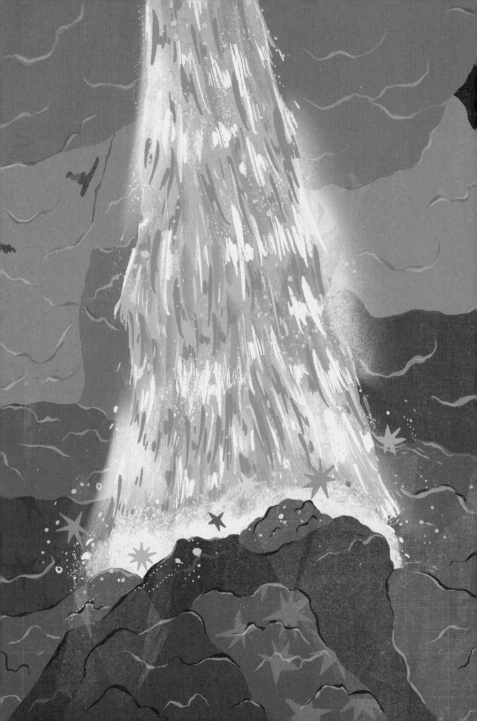

You're as refreshing as
a waterfall, and as exciting
as standing behind one.

I like you more than
inside jokes in
lofty treehouses...

...and dandelion wishes

and whispered secrets.

You're as adventurous as a train,
just pulling out of the station,
blowing its horn adieu.

I like you more than
drinks with fancy umbrellas
and bites on tiny toothpicks...

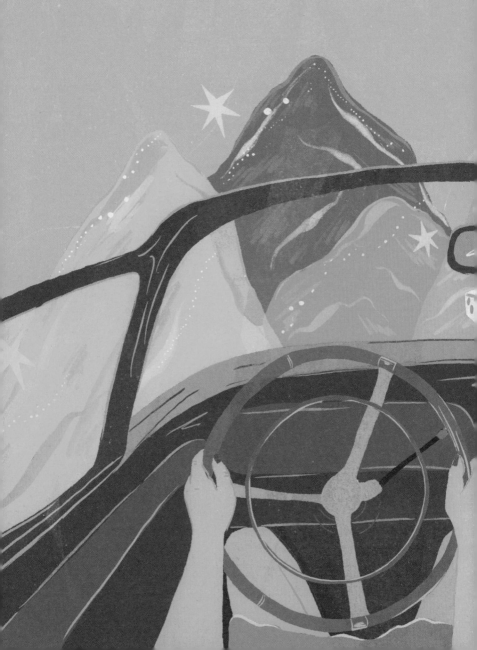

...more than a long road trip

with the rooftop wide open.

You're as generous
as samples at a market.

As soothing as a quiet
bookshop downtown.

COFFEE SHOP

I like you more than hearing
musicians tune up for a concert...

...while wearing the
comfiest shirt, sitting in
the fluffiest grass.

You're as bright as a lemonade stand
with scooters parked nearby.

I like you more than
summer evenings in the park...

...and chasing bubbles in the air.

You are as thoughtful
as a get-well note

or a package left
on a doorstep.

I like you more than biscuits,
still warm from the oven...

...more than fuzzy socks
and hot soup on a frosty day.

You're as freeing as a forward fold,
as comforting as a child's pose.

I like you more than dancing in slippers,

and then sliding into a freshly made bed.

You're as terrific as a sunset,
as trusty as a robe.

It's amazing, really.

While there are a million different delights in the world,

I like *you* the very best.

COMPENDIUM.
live inspired

Written by: Miriam Hathaway
Illustrated by: Flor Fuertes
Edited by: Amelia Riedler
Art Directed by: Megan Gandt

Library of Congress Control Number: 2022933397 | ISBN: 978-1-970147-79-7

1st printing. Printed in China with soy inks on FSC®-Mix certified paper.

*Create
meaningful
moments
with gifts
that inspire.*

CONNECT WITH US
live-inspired.com | sayhello@compendiuminc.com

   @compendiumliveinspired
#compendiumliveinspired